TASTES LIKE SCHMIDT

THE UNOFFICIAL
NEW GIRL COOKBOOK

RECIPES FROM THE LOFT

"IT COMBINES THE RECIPES WITH THE SHOW IN THE MOST CREATIVE WAY. IT'S LIKE YOU'RE WALKING DOWN MEMORY LANE AS YOU READ THROUGH THE COOKBOOK - WARNING, IT WILL MAKE YOU WANT TO RE-WATCH IMMEDIATELY!"

-AMAZON CUSTOMER

"THERE IS SOMETHING FOR EVERY LOFT 4D RESIDENT AT HEART WITHIN THESE PAGES. THIS COOKBOOK HAS FOOD FOR EVERY SITUATION: TRYING IMPRESS YOUR FRIENDS, EATING LIKE MEN, BAKING YOUR TEARS AWAY, OR GENTLY LETTING SOMEONE DOWN WITH FRIENDLY CORNBREAD, THIS IS THE COOKBOOK FOR YOU."

-WHITNEY MEADS

"I'VE NEVER SMILED/LAUGHED MY WAY THROUGH A COOKBOOK, NOR READ ONE SO QUICKLY. THE CREATIVE TITLES, NOSTALGIC QUOTES, AND SIMPLE DESIGN MAKE THIS COOKBOOK PERFECT FOR NEW GIRL LOVERS - NO MUSS, NO FUSS JUST DAMN GOOD FOOD WITH LAUGHS TO BOOT!"

-B&A

DEDICATED TO THE DESSERT-PEOPLE,
THE NON-DESSERT-PEOPLE,
THE DEPRESSION-ERA GARBAGE MEN,
THE NUTMEG SALESMEN, THE PRANK SINATRAS,
THE SIG OTHS', THE ZANIACS,
THE SLOW PUZZLERS, THE STREET YOUTHS,
AND THOSE WHO ROCK A LOT OF POLKA DOTS.

"I WOULD REALLY APPRECIATE IT IF YOUR NON-TAHITIAN VANILLA WAS NOT TOUCHING MY TAHITIAN VANILLA."

RECIPES

APPETIZERS

Cheddar Pop-o-Corno
Mozzarella Sticks for Fingers
Murderous Soft Pretzels
Pour Some Sugar on Meatballs
Men of Means Lobster Puffs
Shrimp Forks
The Jaipur-Aviv Spicy Lentil Dip and Challah

BREAKFAST

Miller Family Bacon Fried in Butter
Schmidt's Yogurt Thing
The Morning After Breakfast
Not Cold Toaster Waffles
Unemployment Egg Pie
Mama Gets Her Biscuits
Outside Dave's Banana Nut Muffins

ENTREES

Jess' Gumbo Pot
Z is for Zombie Bread
Winnie the Fish Tacos
Bertie's Cream-Based Soup
Bob Day's Sandwich
Schmaegalman's Deli Special Soup
Robby's Single's Sliders
Ferguson's Leftover Pasta
Chef Ramsay's Valentine's Scallops
Pink Wine Pasta

SIDES

Friendship Cornbread
Brown Sugar Stuffing
Gay Wolf Chinese Food Egg Drop Soup
Honey Roasted Carrots

DRINKS

Reagan's Old Fashioned
The Temple Grandin
Nick's Fruity Drinks
Hand Bell-inis
The True American
Julius Pepperwood's Chicago Mule
Ma Called, the Bees are Back!

DESSERTS

The Caramel Miracle
Gave Me Cookie, Got You Cookie
Jess's Birthday Cake
Not a Dessert Person Cupcakes
Loft Buttercream
Dr. Sam's Brownies
The Bearclaw
Dead Dad Card-amom Cookies

EXTRAS

Mango Chut-uh-ney
The Sauce
Ms. Day's Jamboree Jam
The Griffin's Bar Mix
Monkey, Monkey, Where You
Keep Your Crackers

APPETIZERS

CHEDDAR POP-O-CORNO

It's popcorn in Italian.

SERVES 6

INGREDIENTS

6 tbsp melted butter
1/2 cup cheddar cheese powder
1/4 tsp mustard powder
6 cups popped popcorn or 1/3 cups popcorn kernels
1/2 tsp salt

DIRECTIONS

Put popcorn kernels in a medium brown paper bag and roll the top of it closed. Microwave until the kernels stop popping at the rate of at least 1 per second.

In a large brown paper bag, combine the popcorn and butter by shaking the bag while pouring the butter in a slow stream. Roll the top closed and shake well.

Combine the cheddar cheese powder, mustard powder, and salt in a small bowl. Sprinkle over the popcorn while shaking the bag. Roll the top closed once more and shake vigorously.

Best enjoyed immediately and while watching Italy on Ice.

MOZZARELLA STICKS FOR FINGERS

They make it hard to wrap gifts, but they're delicious.

SERVES 8

INGREDIENTS

2 eggs, beaten
¼ cup water
1 ½ cups Italian seasoned bread crumbs
½ tsp garlic salt
⅔ cup all-purpose flour
⅓ cup cornstarch
1 quart canola oil for deep frying
1 (16 ounce) package mozzarella cheese sticks

DIRECTIONS

Mix the eggs and water together in a small bowl.

Mix the bread crumbs and garlic salt in a medium bowl. In a medium bowl, blend the flour and cornstarch. In a large, heavy saucepan, heat the oil to 365 degrees F.

Working one by one, coat each mozzarella stick in the flour mixture, followed by the egg mixture, then in the bread crumbs and then into the oil.

Fry until golden brown, about 30 seconds. Remove from heat and drain on paper towels.

Eat immediately and though it will be tempting, don't use them to wrap secret santa presents with.

MURDEROUS SOFT PRETZELS

A much better alternative to murder.

MAKES 12 PRETZELS

INGREDIENTS

1 (.25 ounce) package
active dry yeast
2 tbsp brown sugar
1 1/8 tsp salt
1 ½ cups warm water
(110F)
3 cups all-purpose
flour
1 cup bread flour
2 cups warm water
(110 degrees F/45
degrees C)
2 tbsp baking soda
2 tbsp butter, melted
2 tbsp coarse, kosher
salt

DIRECTIONS

Dissolve the yeast, brown sugar, and salt in 1 1/2 cups warm water in a large mixing bowl. Stir in both flours and knead using a stand mixer with a dough hook until dough is elastic and smooth. If kneading by hand, knead dough on a floured surface for about 8 minutes.

Place in a greased bowl, and turn the dough to lightly coat the surface. Cover, and let rise for sixty minutes.

Meanwhile, add 2 cups warm water and baking soda in a wide shallow container. This will be used to briefly dip pretzels in, so the wider the container the easier this will be. Lightly grease some baking sheets. After dough has risen, cut into 12 pieces. Roll each piece into a thin rope. Twist into a pretzel shape, and dip into the baking soda solution. Transfer to a paper towel briefly to absorb excess moisture, then quickly flip onto a greased baking sheet. Let rise for another 15 to 20 minutes.

Preheat an oven to 450 degrees F. Bake in the preheated oven for 8 to 10 minutes, or until golden brown. Brush with melted butter, and sprinkle with coarse salt. Best eaten when it's that time of the month.

POUR SOME SUGAR ON MEATBALLS

A gentlemen's club classic.

___

MAKES 30 MEATBALLS

INGREDIENTS

1 1lb ground beef
1/2 lb ground pork
1/2 cup panko bread crumbs
1/2 cup shredded parmesan cheese
1 egg
2 cloves garlic, grated
1/2 tsp salt
1/2 tsp pepper

Sauce:
2-3 tbsp water
1/2 cup brown sugar
1/2 cup barbecue sauce
1-2 tsp chili flakes

DIRECTIONS

In a large mixing bowl, mix all meatball ingredients together. Using a cookie scoop or spoon, scoop balls of the mixture and roll by hand to form.

Set aside and heat a large, oiled skillet. Place the meatballs in the skillet one by one. After they cook for about 4 minutes, flip the meatballs and cook an additional 4 minutes. Making sure none are stuck to the bottom, start tossing them in the pan a little more to cook them evenly. Cook in batches as necessary. With all of the cooked meatballs in the pan, drain the fat, leaving a few tablespoons' worth in the pan. Add 2 tablespoons of water to deglaze the pan, scraping up any stuck-on pieces. Add the sugar, adding additional tablespoons of water if the pan looks too dry.

The sauce will begin to thicken and bubble to a medium brown color.

Remove from heat and add in the barbecue sauce and chili flakes to taste. Stir well and serve.

MEN OF MEANS LOBSTER PUFFS

You'll feel rich in dignity and money with this luxurious lunch. Men of means!

MAKES 4-6 PUFFS

INGREDIENTS

3 tbsp butter
3 tbsp thinly sliced green onion
2 tbsp diced red bell pepper
1 rib celery, sliced
3 tbsp all-purpose flour
1/2 tsp seasoning salt
1 1/2 cups whole milk
1 1/2 cups cooked and diced lobster meat
salt and fresh pepper to taste
1/2 cup shredded parmesan cheese
1 tsp chopped parsley
4 to 6 pre-baked puff pastry shells

DIRECTIONS

Melt butter over medium heat in a saucepan; add sliced green onion, bell pepper, and celery. Sauté, stirring until celery is soft.

Sprinkle flour in pan until blended; add seasoned salt.

Add in milk and continue cooking, stirring constantly, until thick. It should begin to bubble. Stir in the Parmesan cheese.

Once cheese is melted, add lobster. Salt and pepper, to taste. Stir in parsley. Turn off the burner and heat the pastry shells.

Spoon the creamed lobster mixture into hot baked puff pastry shells. Garnish with a little more parmesan cheese and parsley, if desired. Serve immediately.

SHRIMP FORKS

Your little, girly hands may be no good for basketball, but they're good for eating shrimp cocktail.

SERVES 4-6

INGREDIENTS

Court Bouillon:
10 cups cold water
2 medium carrots, quartered
2 stalks celery, quartered
1 large onion, quartered
1 head garlic, halved
1 lemon, halved
1/2 bunch parsley
5 sprigs fresh thyme
2 bay leaves

1 lb medium or large shrimp, in the shell, rinsed and de-veined cocktail sauce and lemon wedges to serve

DIRECTIONS

Put the water, carrot, celery, onion, garlic, lemon, parsley, thyme, and bay leaves in a pot and bring to a boil over high heat. Lower the heat to a simmer, set a cover on top slightly ajar, and cook for 10 to 30 minutes.

Drop the shrimp into the liquid and turn off the heat. Cook the shrimp, stirring occasionally, until they curl and turn pink, about 2 to 2 1/2 minutes for medium shrimp, 3 minutes for large ones. Drain and cool to room temperature. Peel the shrimp and remove the vein along the curve of the shrimp, if desired. Refrigerate if not serving right away. If refrigerated, bring the shrimp to room temperature 20 minutes before serving.

To serve put the cocktail sauce in a medium bowl and surround with the shrimp, or loop the shrimp over the edge of an individual cocktail glass and top with the sauce. Garnish with the lemon and serve.

THE JAIPUR-AVIV

Spicy Lentil Dip and Challah fit to christen a new household.

MAKES 2 CUPS OF DIP

INGREDIENTS

For the Lentil Dip:
1 cup red lentils
1 onion, diced
2 ½ cups water
2 tsp curry powder
¾ tsp cayenne
1 tbsp vegetable oil
2 cloves crushed garlic
1 tsp cumin seeds

DIRECTIONS

In a medium saucepan combine the lentils, onion and water. Cover and bring to a boil. Reduce heat to low and simmer for 25 minutes or until lentils are soft. Use an immersion blender to blend the mixture until smooth.

Toast curry powder and cumin seeds in a small skillet on medium until fragrant. Add cayenne, oil and garlic. Saute for 1 minute.

Stir spice mixture into lentils and serve with challah. See next page.

THE JAIPUR-AVIV

Spicy Lentil Dip and Challah fit to christen a new household.

MAKES 2 LOAVES

INGREDIENTS

For the Challah:
¼ cup white sugar
1 tbsp salt
¼ cup vegetable oil
1 ¼ cups warm water
2 (.25 ounce)
packages active dry
yeast
4 eggs
6 cups all-purpose
flour

DIRECTIONS

Place sugar, salt, and oil in large bowl. Add warm water, and stir to dissolve the sugar and salt. Stir in yeast, and let stand until yeast activates and begins to bubble. Add 3 slightly beaten eggs.

Stir 4 1/2 cups of flour into the yeast mixture. Lightly flour a clean surface and dump the dough on top. Work in 1 to 2 cups of flour. Knead until smooth and elastic, about 8 to 10 minutes.

Place dough into a lightly greased bowl. Turn the dough several times to coat the surface. Proof the dough by covering bowl with a damp cloth. Let it rise until doubled in size. Punch it down and allow to rise a second time, about 45 more minutes.

Divide dough in half and divide each half into three equal parts. Make two braids, and place both breads on a greased baking sheet. Cover, and allow to rise until doubled. Beat remaining egg and use this to brush the top of each loaf before baking.

Bake at 350 degrees F (175 degrees C) for 35 minutes until golden brown. Allow loaves to cool on a wire rack.

BREAKFAST

MILLER FAMILY BACON
FRIED IN BUTTER

Is the butter really necessary? Of course not, but at least it won't stick to the pan.

SERVES ONE
MILLER FAMILY

INGREDIENTS

1 lb bacon
1 tbsp butter

DIRECTIONS

Let bacon rest out of the fridge until near room temperature. Heat a cast-iron or other heavy skillet over medium heat and add butter to the pan. When the butter is melted, add bacon strips in a single layer. Cook until browned on bottom, 3 to 4 minutes.

Flip bacon, using tongs, and cook until browned on both sides, about 2 additional minutes.

Drain and reserve fat for another use, and repeat with remaining bacon untill all cooked. Place bacon on a plate lined with puper towels. Serve immediately.

SCHMIDT'S YOGURT THING

Oh the parfait? It's a parfait.

SERVES 1

INGREDIENTS

½ cup sliced
strawberries
½ cup blueberries
½ cup blackberries
6 oz vanilla greek
yogurt
½ banana, sliced
1/3 cup granola

DIRECTIONS

In a tall parfait glass, layer
blackberries, heaping spoonful of the
yogurt, 1/3 of the sliced banana, and
about 2 tablespoons of granola.

Continue to build the parfait, repeating
the layers with strawberries and
blueberries until all of the ingredients
are used completely. Don't serve for
brunch, hybrid meals are for people too
lazy to wake up for a proper breakfast.

THE MORNING AFTER BREAKFAST

We recommend cooking your eggs through, unlike Nick.

SERVES 1

INGREDIENTS

2 eggs
2 tbsp shredded
cheddar cheese
1 tsp heavy whipping
cream
salt and pepper to
taste
½ tsp butter

DIRECTIONS

Whisk eggs together in a small bowl until smooth. Add in cheese, salt, pepper, and heavy cream.

Melt butter in a skillet over medium heat. Pour in egg mixture; cook and stir until set but still moist, 3 to 5 minutes.

Serve with a hand-torn grapefruit and pie.

NOT COLD TOASTER WAFFLES

Man, this waffle had better be hot or I am going Durst on y'all.

SERVES ONE
WINSTON

INGREDIENTS

1 frozen toaster waffle
2 tbsp butter
sprinkle of cinnamon
maple syrup for
serving

DIRECTIONS

Thoroughly butter each side of the waffle and place in a skillet on medium heat. While the first side is cooking, sprinkle the waffle with cinnamon.

Heat each side for approximately 45 seconds. Serve hot with syrup. Whatever you do, serve hot so they don't get hard.

UNEMPLOYMENT EGG PIE

Are you cooking a frittata in a saucepan? What is this? Prison?

SERVES 2

INGREDIENTS

cooking spray
1 tsp olive oil
1 red bell pepper, cut
into thin strips
1 medium white onion,
thinly sliced
¼ cup milk
4 egg whites
2 eggs
½ tsp salt
½ tsp ground black
pepper
1 pinch ground cumin
½ cup salsa

DIRECTIONS

Preheat the oven to 350 degrees F (175 degrees C). Spray a small casserole dish with cooking spray and set aside.

Heat oil in a 12-inch nonstick skillet over medium heat. Add the bell pepper and onion and cook until tender, about 5 minutes.

While pepper and onion are cooking, whisk the milk, egg whites, whole eggs, salt, pepper, and cumin into a medium bowl.

Transfer cooked vegetables to the prepared casserole dish. Top with the egg mixture.

Bake in the preheated oven until the frittata is set, about 30 minutes. Remove friee-tata from the oven and cut into wedges or squares. Place onto a plate and serve with salsa.

MAMA GETS HER BISCUITS

You have to wait until the third date to have these.

MAKES 12 BISCUITS

INGREDIENTS

2 cups all-purpose
flour
½ tsp salt
4 tsp baking powder
½ tsp cream of tartar
2 tsp white sugar
½ cup butter, chilled
and diced
¾ cup milk

DIRECTIONS

Preheat oven to 450 degrees F (230 degrees C).

In a large bowl, whisk dry ingredients together. Using a dough blender or two forks, cut in butter until the mixture forms small pebbles.

Make a well in the center of the dry mixture and pour in the milk. Stir until dough begins to form together. Turn out onto a lightly floured surface.

Press dough together and then roll out until 3/4 inch thick. Use a 2 inch round biscuit cutter to cut rounds out and place on an ungreased baking sheet.

Bake in preheated oven for 10 minutes, or until light golden brown.

OUTSIDE DAVE'S BANANA NUT MUFFINS

So flavorful you can taste it right through the phone.

MAKES 12 MUFFINS

INGREDIENTS

1 1/2 cups all-purpose flour
1 tsp baking powder
1 tsp baking soda
1/2 tsp salt
1 tsp ground cinnamon
1/4 tsp ground nutmeg
3 large ripe bananas
6 tbsp unsalted butter, melted
2/3 cup packed brown sugar
1 large egg, at room temperature
1 tsp pure vanilla extract
2 tbsp milk
1 cup chopped walnuts or pecans

DIRECTIONS

Preheat oven to 425°F Line a 12-count muffin pan with muffin liners.

In a medium bowl, whisk the flour, baking powder, baking soda, salt, cinnamon, and nutmeg together. With a stand mixer or hand mixer and large bowl, mash the bananas. On medium speed, beat in the melted butter, brown sugar, egg, vanilla extract, and milk.

Pour the dry ingredients into the wet ingredients in two parts, then beat until combined. Fold in the walnuts or pecans.

Spoon the batter into liners, filling them all the way to the top. Bake for 5 minutes at 425 then reduce the oven temperature to 350°F. Bake for an additional 16-18 minutes or until a toothpick inserted in the center comes out clean. Don't forget to register to vote.

Allow the muffins to cool for 5 minutes in the muffin pan, then transfer to a wire rack to continue cooling.

ENTREES

JESS' GUMBO POT

Ugh. Gumbo pot? Get out.

MAKES 20 SERVINGS
INGREDIENTS

1 cup all-purpose flour
3/4 cup bacon drippings
1 cup coarsely chopped celery
1 large onion, coarsely chopped
1 large green bell pepper, coarsely chopped
2 cloves garlic, minced
1 pound andouille sausage, sliced
3 quarts water
6 cubes beef bouillon
1 tbsp white sugar
salt to taste
2 tbsp hot sauce
4 bay leaves
½ tsp dried thyme leaves
1 (14.5 ounce) can stewed tomatoes
1 (6 ounce) can tomato sauce
2 tsp file powder, divided
2 tbsp bacon drippings
2 (10 ounce) packages frozen cut okra, thawed
2 tbsp distilled white vinegar
1 lb lump crab meat
3 lb uncooked medium shrimp, peeled and deveined
2 tbsp Worcestershire sauce

DIRECTIONS

Make a roux by whisking the flour and bacon drippings together in a large, heavy saucepan over medium-low heat to form a smooth mixture. Cook the roux by whisking frequently until it turns a rich brown color, 20-30 minutes. Watch heat and whisk constantly to avoid burning the roux. Remove from heat; continue whisking until mixture cools.

Add the celery, onion, green bell pepper, and garlic into the work bowl of a food processor. Pulse until the vegetables are finely chopped. Mix the vegetables into the roux, and stir in the sausage. Over medium-low heat, bring the mixture to a simmer. Cook until vegetables are tender, 10-15 minutes. Remove from heat, and set aside.

In large pot, add the water and beef bouillon cubes to a boil. Stir until the bouillon cubes dissolve, then add the roux mixture into the boiling water. Reduce to a simmer, then add the sugar, salt, hot sauce, bay leaves, thyme, stewed tomatoes, and tomato sauce. Simmer over low heat for 1 hour; mix in 2 teaspoons of file gumbo powder at the 45-minute mark.

Meanwhile, melt 2 tbsp bacon drippings in a skillet. Cook the okra with vinegar over medium heat for 15 minutes. Remove okra with a slotted spoon, and stir into the simmering gumbo. Mix in crab meat, shrimp, and Worcestershire sauce, and simmer for 45 more minutes. Just before serving, stir in 2 more teaspoons of file gumbo powder. Serve over rice.

Z IS FOR ZOMBIE BREAD

Zombie zoo, zombie zoo. Who let them zombies out that damn Zombie Zoo?
A cheese zombie is a regional delicacy, and Nick would definitely be into it.

FEEDS ONE
HUNGRY HORDE

INGREDIENTS

2 3/4 tbsp active dry yeast
3/4 cup warm water
6 1/2 cups all purpose or bread flour
1/3 cup non-instant nonfat dry milk
7 tbsp granulated sugar
7 tbsp vegetable oil
1 1/2 cups water (at 68 degrees)
1 1/4 pounds American cheese, sliced
1/2 tbsp melted butter

DIRECTIONS

Dissolve dry yeast in warm water to activate. Set aside.

Place flour, dry milk, sugar, and salt in mixer. Using a dough hook, blend on low speed for 2 minutes.

Add vegetable oil continue to mix on low speed 2 more minutes. Add water and continue blending for another minute. Add yeast mixture and mix 2 minutes.

Once fully incorporated, knead the dough on medium speed until the dough is smooth and elastic, about 8 minutes. Divide dough into two equal pieces and place in a warm area to proof (about 90 degrees) for 45-60 minutes.

Use pan spray to lightly grease a half-sheet pan and evenly stretch one dough ball on pan. Layer cheese slices across dough, then take second dough ball and stretch evenly on the top to sandwich the cheese inside the layers of dough. Place back in the warm area until doubled in size, 30-50 minutes.

Pre-heat over to 400 degrees F. Bake until lightly brown for 18-20 minutes in a conventional oven. While the cheese zombies are still warm, brush lightly with melted butter.

Serve along with tomato soup.

WINNIE THE FISH TACOS

Why have the Main Stage strip club tacos when you can have these instead?

SERVES 8

INGREDIENTS

1 cup all-purpose flour
2 tbsp cornstarch
1 tsp baking powder
½ tsp salt
1 egg
1 cup beer
½ cup plain yogurt
½ cup mayonnaise
1 lime, juiced
1 minced jalapeno pepper
1 tsp minced capers
½ tsp dried oregano
½ tsp ground cumin
½ tsp dried dill weed
1 tsp cayenne pepper
1 quart frying oil
1 pound cod fillets in 2 to 3 ounce portions
1 (12 ounce) package corn tortillas
½ medium head cabbage, finely shredded

DIRECTIONS

First, make the beer batter. In a large bowl, add the flour, cornstarch, baking powder, and salt. In a separate small bowl, combine the egg and beer, then stir into the flour mixture (don't worry about a few lumps).

Next, make the sauce. In a medium bowl, add together the yogurt and mayonnaise and mix until fully incorporated. Slowly stir in fresh lime juice until consistency is slightly runny. Next, add the jalapeno, capers, oregano, cumin, dill, and cayenne.

Heat oil in deep-fryer to 375 degrees F.

Dip the fish pieces in flour, covering both sides. Dip into beer batter then fry until golden brown. Drain the excess oil on the paper towels. Lightly fry tortillas to light brown. To serve, place fried fish in a tortilla, and add shredded cabbage on top. Finish with adding the sauce.

BERTIE'S CREAM-BASED SOUP

She is making 10 or 11 soups, and all of them are cream-based. Use this soup base to make what ever kind of soup you want.

SERVES 6

INGREDIENTS

½ cup unsalted butter
6 tbsp all-purpose flour
2 cups milk
2 cubes chicken bouillon
freshly ground black
pepper
salt

DIRECTIONS

Add butter to a medium saucepan. Once melted, add flour and make a roux. Add milk and bouillon cubes. Cook over low heat until thick.

To this base you can add whatever ingredients you'd like, or use as a substitute for Cream of Whatever Soup in other recipes. Cooked vegetables, meat, or cheese in whatever combination can be added. Add more milk to adjust thickness.

Ideas:

- steamed broccoli and cheddar cheese
- chunks of baked potato with cheese, bacon pieces, and green onion
- roasted and pureed tomatoes for a bisque
- chunks of roasted potatoes and leeks
- steamed asparagus cut in pieces topped with grated cheese and bacon pieces

Add salt and pepper to taste. Wash down with a swig of your stomach medicine.

BOB DAY'S SANDWICH

Lettuce, tomato, lettuce, meat, meat, meat, meat, meat, cheese, lettuce.

MAKES 1 SANDWICH

INGREDIENTS

2 slices sandwich
bread
3 pieces of lettuce
5 slices of meat
tomato slices
sliced cheese
mayonnaise
mustard
salt and pepper to
taste

DIRECTIONS

Toast your bread, then layer some
lettuce, then tomato, followed by more
lettuce and then meat, meat, meat,
meat, meat, cheese, and lettuce.

Add mayo, mustard, salt, and pepper.

You are a sandwich genius.

SCHMAEGALMAN'S DELI SPECIAL SOUP

Thankfully you don't have to wait in line or punch the city in the damn throat for this special soup.

SERVES 6

INGREDIENTS

1 whole chicken, about 5 lbs
1 yellow onion, chopped
8 carrots, peeled and sliced
1 chopped parsnip, peeled and woody core removed
2 stalks celery, chopped
1 bunch fresh dill weed, chopped, or 1 Tbs dried dill (optional)
2 cloves garlic, crushed
salt and pepper to taste

2 cups matzo meal
6 eggs
6 tbsp vegetable oil
2 tsp salt

DIRECTIONS

Add the whole chicken in a large pot with the breast side down. Fill with cool water to fill the pot, leaving 3 inches of room. Make sure chicken is completely covered. Add the onion, carrot, parsnip, celery and dill (if using). Simmer but do not boil. Cook over medium heat half covered for 2 hours.

Skim the fat from the top of the soup, then add the garlic. Partially cover again, and simmer for an additional 2 hours.

In a medium bowl, stir the matzo meal, eggs, oil, salt, and 1/4 cup cooled soup broth. Refrigerate mixture for 20 minutes.

Fill a large pot halfway full of water and bring to a boil. Divide the matzoh mix into four pieces, then each piece into four more pieces, making 16 balls in total. Use wet hands to keep the dough from sticking while rolling into spheres. Lower the matzoh balls into boiling water, cover, and cook for about 35 minutes.

While the matzo balls are cooking, remove the bones and skin from the chicken. Cut into pieces, then return to the soup. Serve the matzo balls in a bowl of the hot chicken soup.

ROBBY'S SINGLE'S SLIDERS

The trick is to take the meat from three different sliders, and then just sort of mash 'em into one big boy that stands on his own.

MAKES 24 SLIDERS

INGREDIENTS

2 lbs ground beef (80/20)
1 (1 1/4 oz) envelope dry onion soup mix
2 tbsp Worcestershire
2 tbsp ketchup
2 12 packs of Original Hawaiian Sweet Rolls, cut in half

DIRECTIONS

Preheat your grill. This ensures that your grill will be nice and hot when it's time to cook your sliders.

In a large bowl, add ground beef, soup mix, worcestershire, and ketchup. Mix with clean hands or a wooden spoon.

Form the slider patties. Grab a small chunk of the ground beef and shape the patties using your hands. You can make them thick or thin. Let them rest at least 10 minutes before grilling.

Throw your slider patties on the grill and cook for about 2-3 minutes per side. If adding cheese, do so during the last minute of grilling and keep the grill closed.

Serve sliders on rolls with your choice of toppings.

FERGUSON'S LEFTOVER PASTA

Best eaten with your cat.

SERVES 6

INGREDIENTS

2 skinless, boneless
chicken breast halves
4 cloves minced garlic
8 ounce package
uncooked rigatoni pasta
6 slices bacon
1 tbsp vegetable oil
2 small zucchini or yellow
squash, or combo, sliced
1 cup Alfredo sauce
¼ cup milk
6 sun-dried tomatoes,
softened and chopped
3 tbsp Parmesan cheese
¼ cup sliced almonds

DIRECTIONS

Preheat oven to 350 degrees F (175 degrees C). Lightly grease a baking dish.

Place the chicken in the prepared baking dish, and coat with the minced garlic. Bake 25 minutes, or until chicken reaches 165 degrees F internally. Let cool and chop into small pieces.

Bring a large pot of salted water to a boil. Add the rigatoni, cook until al dente (about 10 minutes), and drain.

Over medium-high heat, cook bacon in a skillet until evenly brown. Drain on paper towels and once cool, crumble the bacon into pieces.

In the same pan with bacon grease, heat over medium heat, and saute the zucchini/yellow squash until tender and lightly browned.

In a small bowl, mix the Alfredo sauce and milk. Add the chicken to the cooked pasta. Pour in the Alfredo sauce followed by the squash. Sprinkle with sun-dried tomatoes, bacon, Parmesan cheese, and almonds. Eat immediately or refrigerate and enjoy tomorrow with your cat.

CHEF RAMSAY'S VALENTINE'S DAY SCALLOPS

Do not serve these to liars.

SERVES 4

INGREDIENTS

1 pound scallops
salt and freshly ground
black pepper to taste
2 tbsp AP flour
2 tbsp butter
1 tbsp pesto
1 tbsp capers
1 cup heavy whipping
cream
1/2 cup chicken broth

DIRECTIONS

Season scallops with salt and pepper on both sides, then dredge in flour.

Melt butter in a skillet over medium heat. Add scallops and cook briefly on each side, about 1 to 2 minutes per side.

Add pesto and capers; mix well. Stir in heavy cream and broth and bring to a boil. Remove from heat and serve.

Pair with a rosé, crusty bread, sauteed asparagus to curb the loneliness.

PINK WINE PASTA

Is this pasta sauce made with bath water? Might as well be, it's made with rosé.

SERVES 8

INGREDIENTS

3 tbsp olive oil
½ tsp dried basil
½ tsp dried thyme
½ tsp dried oregano
½ tsp dried parsley
¼ tsp dried red pepper flakes
2 tbsp minced onion
2 tbsp minced green bell pepper
1 tbsp minced garlic
8 ounces tomato sauce
½ tsp chicken soup base
1 tsp white sugar
1 pound cheese tortellini
8 oz heavy cream
½ cup rosé wine

DIRECTIONS

In a large skillet, heat olive oil over medium-low heat and add basil, thyme, oregano, parsley and dried red pepper flakes; stir together for 5-7 minutes until aromatic.

Add onion, bell pepper, and garlic. Cook until onions are translucent; add tomato sauce and bring to a boil, stirring well. Add chicken bouillon and sugar; stir.

While the sauce is cooking, bring to boil a large pot of salted water. Add tortellini and cook according to the package directions. Drain and set aside.

Reduce heat on the sauce and add cream and wine. Bring to a simmer, stirring constantly and then turn off heat. Add pasta and serve, but be careful...pink wine makes me...well, you know.

SIDES

FRIENDSHIP CORNBREAD

Chocolate's way too sexual. This is just good, old-fashioned Kansas cornbread.

MAKES APPROX. 15 SERVINGS

INGREDIENTS

1 ½ cups cornmeal
2 ½ cups milk
2 cups all-purpose flour
1 tbsp baking powder
1 tsp salt
⅔ cup white sugar
2 eggs
½ cup vegetable oil

DIRECTIONS

Preheat oven to 400 degrees F.

In a small bowl, combine cornmeal and milk; let sit for 5 minutes. Grease a 9x13 inch baking pan.

In a large bowl, add flour, baking powder, salt, sugar, and whisk. Mix in the cornmeal mixture. Add eggs and oil and mix until smooth. Pour batter into prepared pan.

Bake in preheated oven for 30 to 35 minutes, or until a knife inserted into the center of the cornbread comes out clean.

Let cool completely, then give it to your ex.

BROWN SUGAR STUFFING

The secret is a pinch of brown sugar, and then...a couple more handfuls of brown sugar.

MAKES 8 SERVINGS

INGREDIENTS

1 cup diced onion
½ cup butter
1 cup cranberries
2 tbsp brown sugar
2 tsp dried rosemary
½ tbsp dried sage
½ cup fresh orange juice
8 slices raisin bread and 6 slices whole wheat bread, cut into 1/2 cubes and toasted
½ cup vegetable broth

DIRECTIONS

Preheat oven to 325 degrees F (165 degrees C).

Cook diced onion in butter over low heat until soft, but not transluscent. Add cranberries, brown sugar, rosemary and sage, orange juice. Salt and pepper to taste.

In a large bowl, add bread cubes. Add the onion-cranberry-herb mixture, and mix thoroughly.

Spoon into buttered 3 or 4 quart casserole, drizzle with broth, dot with butter. Cover with tinfoil. Bake for 30 minutes. Uncover the casserole dish and bake an additional 30 minutes.

GAY WOLF CHINESE FOOD EGG DROP SOUP

"Wait. I'm a gay wolf too. Would you like to eat some wolf chinese food?"

SERVES 1

INGREDIENTS

1 cup chicken broth
¼ tsp soy sauce
¼ tsp sesame oil
1 tsp cornstarch
2 tsp water
1 egg, beaten
1 tsp chopped fresh chives or green onion
⅛ tsp salt
¼ tsp ground white pepper

DIRECTIONS

In a small saucepan, combine the chicken broth, soy sauce and sesame oil. Bring to a boil.

In a separate bowl, stir together the cornstarch and water. Stir to fully dissolve cornstarch. Pour into the boiling broth. Turn off the heat.

Stir gently the mixture in the saucepan while you pour in the egg. Season with chives or green onion, salt and pepper before serving.

HONEY ROASTED CARROTS

They're like regular roasted carrots, but you say sweet things to them while you're roasting them.

MAKES 4 SERVINGS

INGREDIENTS

8 carrots, peeled
3 tbsp olive oil
¼ cup honey
salt and ground black
pepper to taste

DIRECTIONS

Preheat an oven to 350 degrees F (175 degrees C).

Place the peeled whole carrots into a baking dish. Drizzle with olive oil. Mix until the carrots are completely coated. Drizzle the honey over the carrots, then season to taste with salt and pepper; mix until evenly coated.

Bake in the preheated oven until just tender, or cooked to your desired degree of doneness, 40 minutes to 1 hour.

DRINKS

REAGAN'S OLD FASHIONED

"It's a perfect Old Fashioned."
"I know."

MAKES ONE COCKTAIL

INGREDIENTS

1 sugar cube
3 dashes Angostura bitters
Couple drops of water
2 ounces bourbon
Garnish: orange peel and a Luxardo cherry

DIRECTIONS

Add the sugar cube and bitters to a rocks glass, then add water, and stir until sugar is nearly dissolved
Fill the glass with large ice cubes, add the bourbon, and gently stir to combine.
Express the oil of an orange peel over the glass, then drop in. Add the cherry and serve.

THE
TEMPLE GRANDIN

The perfect drink if you want to feel friendly and compassionate.

MAKES FOUR COCKTAILS

INGREDIENTS

Ice
3 cups lemon-lime soda
Juice of 1 lime
4 tsp. grenadine
6 oz coconut rum
Maraschino cherries and a
squeeze of lemon for
serving

DIRECTIONS

Fill 4 glasses with ice. In a pitcher, mix soda, lime juice, and coconut rum. Divide between glasses and top each glass off with grenadine. Serve with a maraschino cherry and a squeeze of lemon.

NICK'S
FRUITY DRINKS

It's like an explosion of fruit. Look at you being so naughty.

SERVES 1

INGREDIENTS

2 ounces pineapple
juice
2 ounces cranberry
juice
1 ounce coconut rum
Squeeze of lime
Splash of grenadine
Optional:
Orchid
maraschino cherry
pineapple slice
tiny umbrella

DIRECTIONS

Combine all ingredients in a shaker
with ice. Serve over ice in a glass or a
coconut & garnish with orchid,
maraschino cherry, pineapple slice, and
tiny umbrella. Drink through a crazy
straw if you want things to get weird.

HAND BELL-INIS

It's pa-rest-pa-pa-pa-rest-pa-pa-pa-rest-pa-pa-paaaaaaa. Forget it. Just trade your hand bells in for these bellinis.

MAKES 4 COCKTAILS

INGREDIENTS

1 bag of frozen peaches
1 bottle of Prosecco

DIRECTIONS

Thaw the bag of sliced peaches, either at room temperature (it will take 3 to 4 hours) or in the refrigerator overnight.

Blend the defrosted peaches in a blender or food processor.
Pour 1/4 cup of the chilled purée into a champagne flute.

Pour in some chilled Prosecco, being careful not to overflow the glass.
Using your dominant bell hand, gently stir to combine.

Top off the drink with another splash of Prosecco. Serve at once!

THE TRUE AMERICAN

So it's 50% drinking game, 50% life-sized Candyland. More like 75% drinking, 25% Candyland. By the way, the floor is molten lava.

SERVES 1

INGREDIENTS

1 beer of your choice

DIRECTIONS

Open the beer and always keep it in your hand. That's it. Replace as needed.

One, two, three, four!
JFK! FDR!

JULIUS PEPPERWOOD'S CHICAGO MULE

Perfect to serve with deep-dish pizza. Thin crust? No thank you. I'm from Chicago.

SERVES 1 LONELY EX-COP/MARINE

INGREDIENTS

2 oz pepper vodka
1 ginger beer
1 dried chili
1 lemon wedge

DIRECTIONS

Fill a mule mug with ice cubes, add 2 oz of pepper vodka. Top off with ginger beer. Garnish with the dried chili and lemon wedge. Enjoy as you work on your creative writing class homework and/or solve crimes.

MA CALLED, THE BEES ARE BACK!

The perfect drink to have if you want to escape a bad date.

MAKES 2 COCKTAILS

INGREDIENTS

1 ounce honey syrup
2 ounces lemon juice (about 1 medium lemon)
4 ounces gin
Lemon twist, for garnish

DIRECTIONS

To make the honey syrup: Combine equal parts honey and water (2 tablespoons each if you're only making a few cocktails) in a microwave-safe bowl. Warm in the microwave just until you can completely stir the honey into the water. Set aside.

Before juicing your lemons, use a vegetable peeler or channel knife to peel off two strips of zest for your twist.

Add the honey syrup, lemon juice and gin to a cocktail shaker with ice Shake well and strain the drink into two martini glasses.

Twist the lemon peel over the cocktail to release some of its oils, then drop it in. Enjoy while cold.

DESSERT

THE CARAMEL MIRACLE

The perfect baby shower dessert.

MAKES 80 CARAMEL SHORTBREAD SQUARES

INGREDIENTS

1 1/3 cup butter,
softened, plus 1 cup, plus
1 tbsp
1/2 cup white sugar
2 1/2 cups all-purpose
flour
1 cup packed light
brown sugar
4 tbsp light corn syrup
1 cup sweetened
condensed milk
2 1/2 cups semisweet
chocolate chips

DIRECTIONS

Preheat oven to 350 degrees F (175 C).

In a medium bowl, mix together 1 1/3 cup butter, white sugar, and flour until evenly crumbly. Press into a 9x13 inch baking pan lined with parchment paper. Bake for 20 minutes. Pop the shortbread into the freezer while you continue making the caramel.

In a large saucepan, combine 1 cup butter, brown sugar, corn syrup, and sweetened condensed milk. Set burner to medium-low and slowly bring to a boil. Continue to boil for 5 minutes stirring constantly. Remove from heat and beat vigorously with a wooden spoon for about 3 minutes. Pour over baked crust. Cool in the fridge until it begins to firm while you heat the chocolate.

Put chocolate and the last tablespoon of butter in a microwave-safe bowl. Heat for 1 minute, then stir and continue to heat and stir at 20-second intervals until chocolate is melted and smooth. Pour chocolate over the caramel layer and spread evenly to cover. Let chill completely before cutting into squares.

GAVE ME COOKIE, GOT YOU COOKIE

You wanna mama-bird me the cookie?

MAKES 18 COOKIES

INGREDIENTS

3/4 cup butter, softened
3/4 cup white sugar
1 egg
1 1/2 cups all-purpose flour
1/2 cup cornmeal
1 tsp baking powder
1/4 tsp salt
1 tsp vanilla extract
1/2 cup raisins (optional)

DIRECTIONS

In a large bowl, cream the butter and sugar together. Add egg and beat well.

In another bowl, whisk together flour, cornmeal, baking powder and salt. In 3 parts, add the dry ingredients to the butter mixture, fully incorporating before mixing the next part. Add vanilla and blend thoroughly. If adding raisins, stir in now (as I live and breathe.)

Form dough into ball, wrap tightly in plastic wrap, and chill until firm, at least 1 hour.

Flour a surface. Roll out dough to 1/4 inch thickness. Cut with cookie cutters and place 1 inch apart on a lightly greased cookie sheet.

Bake in 350 degree F (175 degrees C) oven for 10-12 minutes or until edges are golden. Let cool slightly, then move to a baking rack.

JESS'S BIRTHDAY CAKE

This cake is so moist, girls are gonna be like: "Ew, why do you say 'moist'? I hate that word."

SERVES 10-12

INGREDIENTS

1 cup butter, room
temperature
2 cups white sugar
1 tsp vanilla extract
4 eggs, separated,
room temperature
3 tsp baking powder
3 cups all-purpose
flour
1 cup milk, room
temperature
1 pinch salt

DIRECTIONS

Preheat oven to 350 degrees F.

Grease and flour one 9x13 inch pan. In a stand mixer or with a hand mixer, cream the butter and sugar together until fluffy, roughly 5 minutes. Add the egg yolks one at a time, thoroughly combining them before adding the next one. Mix in the vanilla extract.

Sift together the baking powder, salt, and flour. Add the flour mixture to the butter/sugar in three batches, alternating with the milk. Mix after each addition. Scrape down the sides and bottom of the bowl and beat for 60 more seconds.

In a separate bowl, beat the egg whites with a dash of salt until stiff peaks form. Fold one-third of the egg whites into the cake batter to lighten it; gently fold in the remaining egg whites. Pour batter into prepared pan.

Bake in preheated oven until a toothpick inserted in the center comes out clean, about 35 minutes. Cool on wire rack.

Frost with Loft Buttercream.

NOT A DESSERT PERSON
CUPCAKES

It's fundamentally strange. Honestly, it's just weird and freaks me out.

MAKES 12 CHOCOLATE CUPCAKES

INGREDIENTS

2 tbsp all-purpose flour
⅙ tsp baking soda
1 ½ tsp baking powder
½ cup and 1 tbsp unsweetened cocoa powder
1 tsp kosher salt
3 tbsp butter, softened
3 tbsp white sugar
2 medium eggs
3/4 tsp vanilla extract
3/4 cup milk

DIRECTIONS

Preheat oven to 350 degrees F (175 degrees C). Line a cupcake pan with liners.

In a medium bowl, add the flour, baking powder, baking soda, cocoa and salt. Whisk until thoroughly mixed.

In a large bowl, cream together the butter and sugar until light and fluffy. Add the eggs one at a time, beating well with each addition, then stir in the vanilla. Add the flour mixture alternately with the milk; beat well. Evenly fill the muffin cups 3/4 full.

Bake for 15 to 17 minutes in the preheated oven, or until a toothpick inserted into the cake comes out clean.

Wait until cupcakes are completely cool before frosting with Loft Buttercream.

LOFT BUTTERCREAM

In a pinch, make this batch of buttercream and smear it on your lips to seduce women.

MAKES ENOUGH TO FROST ONE JESS' BIRTHDAY CAKE OR ONE DOZEN NOT A DESSERT PERSON CUPCAKES

INGREDIENTS

½ cup unsalted butter, softened
1 ½ tsp vanilla extract
2 cups sifted powdered sugar
2 tbsp milk

DIRECTIONS

Cream room temperature butter until smooth and fluffy. Gradually beat in powdered sugar until fully incorporated. Beat in vanilla extract.

Pour in milk and beat for an additional 3 to 4 minutes.

Use to frost Not a Dessert Person Cupcakes or Jess' Birthday Cake.

Optional: reserve 1/2 c frosting and gradually mix in food coloring to your desired shade. Use a piping bag or Ziploc to pipe "See you in hell, Boomer!"

DR. SAM'S BROWNIES

Best baked as an apology gift, best eaten in rage-filled fistfuls.

MAKES 16 BROWNIES

INGREDIENTS

½ cup butter
1 cup white sugar
2 eggs
1 tsp vanilla extract
⅓ cup unsweetened cocoa powder
½ cup all-purpose flour
¼ tsp salt
¼ tsp baking powder

DIRECTIONS

Preheat oven to 350 degrees F.

Grease and flour an 8-inch square pan. In a large saucepan, melt 1/2 cup butter. Remove from heat, and stir in sugar, eggs, and 1 teaspoon vanilla.

Gently stir in 1/3 cup cocoa, 1/2 cup flour, salt, and baking powder. Mix until incorporated, but do not over mix.

Spread batter into prepared pan. Bake for 25 to 30 minutes. Let cool before cutting. Don't bother cutting it into squares.

THE BEARCLAW

This recipe was supposed to be a recipe for a "meat bar" but autocorrect changed it.

MAKES 24 BEAR CLAWS WITH LEFTOVER FILLING

INGREDIENTS

⅓ cup almond paste
2 ¾ cups ground almonds
½ cup white sugar
1 pinch salt
2 tbsp butter
2 egg whites
½ tsp almond extract
2 tsp amaretto liqueur
3 boxes frozen puff pastry, thawed (approx 1lb per box)
1 egg
1 tbsp water
3 tbsp confectioners' sugar for dusting

DIRECTIONS

In a large bowl, beat almond paste with an electric mixer to break it apart. Add the almonds, sugar, and salt; continue to mix until the almond paste is no longer lumpy. Stir in the butter, egg whites, almond extract, and amaretto liqueur on high speed until fluffy. Put mixture into a pastry bag or sturdy ziplock bag and snip the corner off when ready to pipe. Set aside.

On a lightly floured surface, cut each square of puff pastry dough into 4 equal squares. Trim the edges of the dough. Cut the dough in half lengthwise to make two 4 inch wide strips.

Preheat the oven to 400 degrees F (200 degrees C). Line baking sheets with parchment paper.

With a pastry bag, pipe a stripe of filling down the center of each strip. You can also spoon the filling in the middle. Whisk together the egg and water. Brush onto one edge of each square. Fold each strip over the filling and press gently to seal it. Brush each piece with egg wash. Cut 1/2 inch slits into the sealed edge to make the "claws". Place the bear claws at least two inches apart on baking sheets. Refrigerate and repeat with all the dough and filling.

Bake in the preheated oven until pastry is golden brown, 25 to 30 minutes. Cool and dust with confectioners' sugar right before serving.

DEAD DAD CARD-AMOM COOKIES

Best eaten while grieving and wearing your dad's old yellow tracksuit.

MAKES 3 DOZEN COOKIE

INGREDIENTS

2 cups all-purpose flour
½ tsp baking powder
⅛ tsp baking soda
½ tsp salt
½ tsp ground cardamom
⅔ cup unsalted butter, softened
1 cup white sugar
3 ounce cream cheese, softened
3 tbsp almond paste
1 egg
1 tsp vanilla extract
¼ tsp lemon zest

DIRECTIONS

Preheat the oven to 375 degrees F (190 degrees C). Grease cookie sheets.

In a medium bowl, add flour, baking powder, baking soda, salt and cardamom. Whisk until well incorporated.

In a stand mixer or with a medium bowl and a hand mixer, cream together the butter, sugar, cream cheese and almond paste until smooth. Add the egg, vanilla, and lemon zest. Gradually blend in the dry ingredients until well mixed.

Use a cookie scoop or two teaspoons to scoop dough onto the greased cookie sheets.

Bake for 8 to 10 minutes in the preheated oven. Allow cookies to cool on the baking sheet for 5 minutes. Remove and place cookies on a wire rack to cool completely.

EXTRAS

MANGO CHUT-UH-NEY

You'll love this mango chut-uh-ney, but who are you kidding? You love any type of chut-uh-ney.

MAKES 24 SERVINGS OF CHUTNEY

INGREDIENTS

2 tbsp vegetable oil
1 tsp crushed red pepper flakes
1 large sweet onion, minced
4 inch piece fresh ginger root, peeled and minced
1 large yellow bell pepper, diced
3 large ripe mangoes, peeled, pitted, & diced
1 can pineapple tidbits
½ cup brown sugar
1 ½ tbsp curry powder
½ cup apple cider vinegar

DIRECTIONS

Heat the vegetable oil in a large saucepan over medium heat. Add the red pepper flakes and cook until they begin to sizzle, then stir in the minced onion. Reduce the heat to low, cover, and cook. Stir occasionally until the onions have softened, about 15-20 minutes.

Remove the lid, increase the heat to medium. Stir in the ginger and yellow bell pepper. Cook and stir until the ginger is fragrant, about 2 to 3 minutes.

Stir in the mangoes, pineapple tidbits, brown sugar, curry powder, and vinegar. Bring to a simmer, and cook for 30 minutes. Stir occasionally. Cool the chutney completely when done and store it in an airtight container in the refrigerator.

THE SAUCE

Tastes like the inside of a bear. The real sauce is a Miller family secret-so this substitute will have to do.

MAKES 6-8 SERVINGS

INGREDIENTS

1 tbsp olive oil
1 large onion, chopped
3 cloves garlic, minced
1 tsp dried oregano
2 tsp dried basil
½ pound beef neck bones or 2 beef ribs
1 (29 ounce) can tomato sauce
1 (14.5 ounce) can stewed tomatoes
2 (6 ounce) cans tomato paste
pinch baking soda
3 cups water
1 pound lean ground beef

DIRECTIONS

In a large pot saute onion, garlic, oregano and basil in 1 tablespoon of olive oil. Add the neck bones or beef ribs and let simmer with the lid on until the onions are transparent. Note: if using ground beef cook with onion mixture.

Once onions are clear, add the tomato sauce, tomatoes, tomato paste, baking soda, and water. If using meat in your recipe add at this time. Cover and simmer for 3-6 hours, tasting occasionally.

Before serving, remove neck bones and discard.

Batch can be doubled if you have a sauce pot as big as Nick's.

MS. DAY'S JAMBOREE JAM

You need a jar funnel. A canner. Some fresh fruit. Strawberries. Raspberries. Maybe a tayberry. Do you know how time-consuming this is gonna be?

MAKES 80 SERVINGS

INGREDIENTS

2 cups crushed fresh strawberries or other berries
4 cups sugar
1 (1.75 ounce) package dry pectin
½ cup + 2 tbsp water

DIRECTIONS

In a medium bowl, mix crushed strawberries with sugar, and let stand for 10 minutes to thicken.

Meanwhile, mix the pectin into the water in a small saucepan. Bring the mix to a boil over medium-high heat, and boil for 1 minute. Remove from stove.

Stir the boiling water mix into the strawberries. Allow to stand for 3 minutes before pouring into containers.

Place lids on the containers. Freeze portions that will not be used immediately. Store frozen containers until ready to use. Refrigerated or thawed portions should be used within 3 weeks.

GRIFFIN BAR MIX

It's named after the bar, you buffoon!

MAKES 20 SERVINGS

INGREDIENTS

1 cup butter
2 tsp seasoning salt
1 tbsp Worcestershire sauce
3 tsp onion powder
3 tsp garlic powder
2 cups crispy rice cereal squares
2 cups crispy corn cereal squares
2 cups crispy wheat cereal squares
2 cups toasted oat cereal
1 cup mini pretzels
1 cup mixed nuts

DIRECTIONS

Preheat oven to 275 degrees F (135 degrees C).

In a large roasting pan, melt butter. Mix in seasoning salt, Worcestershire sauce, onion powder, and garlic powder.

Stir crispy rice, corn, wheat and oat cereals, pretzels and nuts into the butter mixture and coat well.

Bake uncovered in the preheated oven for 45 minutes, stirring occasionally.

MONKEY, MONKEY, WHERE YOU KEEP YOUR CRACKERS

You are comrade best!

MAKES 3-4 PANS OF CRACKERS

INGREDIENTS

1 3/4 cups whole wheat flour
1 1/2 cups all-purpose flour
1/4 cup grated parmesan (optional)
1/2 tbsp of your favorite herbs (rosemary, thyme, etc)
1/2 tsp garlic salt
1/3 cup olive oil
1 cup water or low sodium broth
coarse kosher salt for sprinkling

DIRECTIONS

Preheat the oven to 350 degrees F (175 degrees C).

In a medium bowl, whisk together the whole wheat flour, all-purpose flour, garlic salt, herbs of choice, and parmesan if using. Pour in the olive oil and water; mix until just incorporated.

On a lightly floured surface, roll out the dough as thin as you can. Place dough on parchment-lined baking sheets, the number will depend on how thin the dough was rolled. Score with a pastry wheel or knife. Prick each cracker with a fork a few times, and sprinkle with salt.

Bake for 15 to 20 minutes in the preheated oven, or until crisp and light brown. Baking time may be different depending on the thickness of the crackers. When the crackers have cooled, remove them from the baking sheet, and separate them into individual crackers.

Excerpt from Zombie Zoo

```
E W I L T I N F I N I T Y J K L L O W
B N A P R D O S L A P I C N I R P B J
A E G O U L O W C C L B A A H O E A B
T M P R E P S U C E R L K S O R P N C
M E R T A C E I C R R G I A I U P G L
A O A L M M E T O H S B D G E L E S I
N H N A E R P C E D E G A T T R R G A
M A K N R E M A E H E B K X R E W I S
O N S D I B P K T S R Y A I N G O V S
B D D I C E I C N T B O I G M E O I S
I B N I A M O I S M E O I R J R D N T
L E R E N I F F I R G R Y J R A Q G R
E L T L O S A N G E L E S S E S R N A
U L F A N C Y M A N E N N K L O F T T
C S K A O R D G N I C N A D Y T R I D
```

DOUCHEBAG JAR
LOFT
PEPPERWOOD
THE BISH
PRINCIPAL
PORTLAND
LOS ANGELES

GRIFFIN
ASS STRAT
DICE
CECE'S BOYS
SWUIT
TRUE AMERICAN
BANGSGIVING

DIRTY DANCING
HANDBELLS
PRANKS
TINFINITY
FANCYMAN
BATMANMOBILE
ENGRAM PATTERSKY

Printed in Great Britain
by Amazon

77127820R00045